DATE DUE

HAMILTON HAMILTON			
MAR 17 2004			
J. MARTIN			
HAMILTON			
	DISCARD		

DEMCO 38-296

SQUEAKING of ART

The Mice Go to the Museum

SQUEAKING of ART

THE MICE GO TO THE MUSEUM

Monica Wellington

Dutton Children's Books • New York

For Lydia

With grateful acknowledgment and thanks to Barbara Baker.
Thank you also to Pat Zybert, Katharine Sands, and Laura Wellington.
And at Dutton Children's Books, thank you to Lucia Monfried, Sara Reynolds,
Laurin Lucaire, Alan Carr, and Diane Giddis.

Copyright © 2000 by Monica Wellington

All rights reserved.

CIP Data is available.

Published in the United States 2000 by Dutton Children's Books,

a division of Penguin Putnam Books for Young Readers

345 Hudson Street, New York, New York 10014

http://www.penguinputnam.com/yreaders/index.htm

Printed in Hong Kong

First Edition

ISBN 0-525-46165-5

1 3 5 7 9 10 8 6 4 2

All possible care and effort have been taken to
list accurately the works of art at the end of this book.
The author wishes to apologize for any errors that
may have inadvertently occurred.

The pictures for this
book were painted
with gouache.

The text is set in
Goudy Sans Bold.

ABOUT THIS BOOK • The museum in this book is an imaginary one, filled with versions of the author's favorite paintings and works of art. Many are famous masterpieces. Some are less well known. In the back of the book you will find a complete list of these works and the places where they are located. Most of them are in museums in major cities around the world. Perhaps you will have the chance to visit some of these museums and to see some of the original work that inspired the paintings in this book.

Children have more fun—and learn more—when they actively participate in the experience of looking at art by talking about what they see rather than by passively receiving information, such as names and dates. This book is meant to help you and your children develop the skills and vocabulary for looking at, talking about, and enjoying art together.

Each gallery in this imaginary museum is devoted to a specific subject or theme. The text in the frame on the wall in each gallery provides introductory background material about this subject. The main text on the bottom of each page poses questions and offers suggestions of things to discuss with children. As you read it, encourage them to find and point to the paintings being talked about, to answer the questions, to add their own comments and observations, and to join in the conversation with the mice and cat. You might spend a lot of time with some pictures and go more quickly over others. How you read this book and get involved with the art is meant to be very flexible.

A visit to this imaginary museum is an introduction to the world of paintings. It offers a beginning for developing a love of art and museum-going in young children.

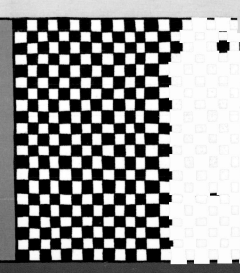

AUTHOR'S NOTE • All my life I have loved going to museums. Now as a parent I love going to museums with my daughter. Museums are wonderful and fun places to explore with children, and I urge you to visit one with your family or with a group. I hope this book inspires you and your children to look at and talk about art with curiosity and imagination. When you go to a museum, you embark on an adventure. Enjoy! And do bring paper and pencils for sketching.

Introduction

Ten mice have come on a trip to the art museum. They go through the doors into the big entrance hall. All of them are talking at once. • **Red** mouse says, "I'm so excited. Where should we start?" • **Blue** mouse picks up a map. "This will help us figure out where to go." • The mice need to buy tickets and check their bags before they go into the galleries. • **Beige** mouse says, "I'm hungry. I need a snack at the café before I do anything."

Coat Check

Rest Rooms

Yellow mouse says, "Let's buy some postcards at the museum shop."
• Purple mouse says, "I'm ready to start looking at the paintings." ᕙᕗ
Another visitor has entered the museum. She is carrying her easel and
box of paints. • Orange mouse says, "I bet that cat is an artist. I wonder
what she is going to do." • "Come with me and see, everybody," says
the cat.

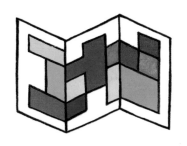

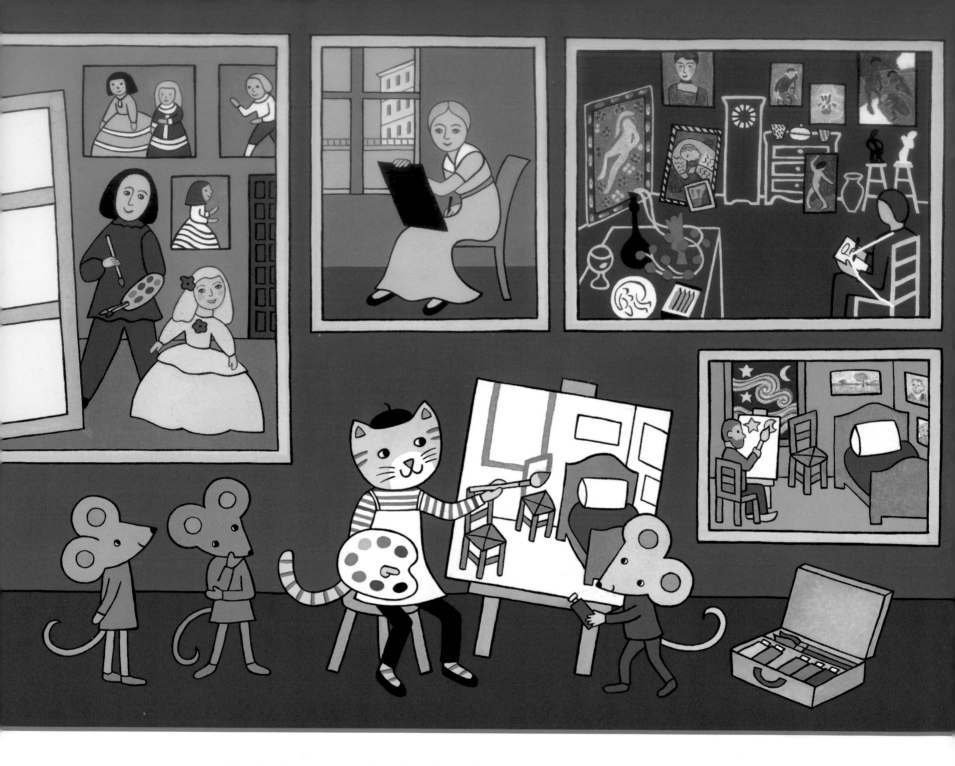

ARTISTS

Find the artists in the paintings. Can you describe what they are doing? What materials are they using? What do their studios look like? Which studio would you like to work in if you were an artist? • **Red** mouse says, "I like the red studio. What a great place to paint pictures full of bright colors." • **Blue** mouse says, "I wonder what that lady is drawing. I wish I

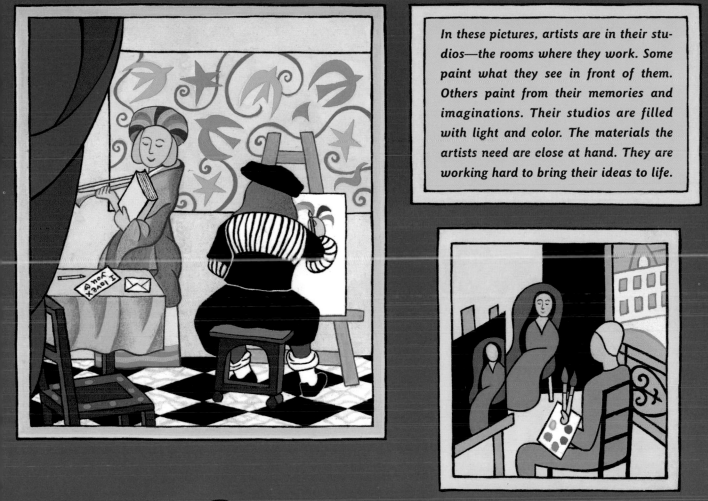

In these pictures, artists are in their studios—the rooms where they work. Some paint what they see in front of them. Others paint from their memories and imaginations. Their studios are filled with light and color. The materials the artists need are close at hand. They are working hard to bring their ideas to life.

could peek over her shoulder and see." • Yellow mouse says, "I see three artists who are painting people from real life." • Purple mouse says, "Looking at all these artists makes me want to sketch right now." • The cat says, "I've always dreamed of being an artist." Look at what she is painting. Guess which is her favorite painting of an artist's studio.

MUSIC AND DANCE

In these pictures, some people are playing instruments, some are dancing, some are listening. Music fills the air. What instruments do you see being played? What do you think the music sounds like in each painting? How would you move to it with your body? • Green mouse says, "In the painting with three musicians, there are jagged edges, zigzag lines, and bright

---

Painters have often shown other creative people in their pictures. These paintings show people playing music and dancing. The musicians make art with the sounds of their instruments. The dancers make art with the movements of their bodies in space. With work, talent, and dedication, artists pursue their art in different ways.

colors. I hear music that is fast and cool." • **Orange** mouse says, "I love the lively music at the circus." • **Pink** mouse says, "The five women look as if they're dancing to happy music. I like dancing with my friends, too." • The cat sways to the music she hears in her imagination. "Guitar music is my favorite." Which painting do you think she is looking at?

CHILDREN PLAYING

Look at all the ways children are playing in these paintings. Try to find the children playing checkers, hoops, and leapfrog. What other activities do you see? How do you think the children feel? Which games look like the most fun to you? • Light Blue mouse says, "I see friends playing cards. One of the players is hiding his cards behind his back. That's not

In these paintings, children are playing in all sorts of ways. Some children are playing games that have rules. Others are not. Some are playing alone. Others are playing with friends. Whether the children are indoors or out, quiet, noisy, or active, they are absorbed in the magic and joy of play.

fair." • **Brown** mouse says, "Look at those kids playing snap-the-whip. We like to do that, too." • **Purple** mouse says, "That girl over there is lucky. The sun is going down, but she gets to play outside late." • The cat is quiet, concentrating hard. "I love to play this game." Can you guess what it is?

The young people in these paintings are all with pets they love and take care of. Animals are fun to play with. However, here the children had to dress up in their best clothes and try to stay still with their pets while the artists painted these important pictures.

What animals do you see in these paintings? What do you think it would be like to have one of these animals as a pet yourself? What do you think it would feel like to hold, to play with, and to take care of? What do you think these children are like as owners? • **Red** mouse says, "Blackbird— watch out! Those cats want to eat you up!" • **Blue** mouse says, "That girl

with the red bows looks bossy, but her dog is cute." • Light Blue mouse
says, "I'm glad I don't have to wear such fancy clothes." • Yellow mouse
says, "I think the little fluffy bird is hurt, and the child is going to help it
get better." • The cat says, "That cat is in the perfect place, nestled right
in the arms of someone who loves her." Which cat is she talking about?

PORTRAITS

How would you describe the people in these pictures? What do they look like? What are they wearing? Who seems happy, serious, scared? What else? Can you pretend you are any of these people and pose as you see them in the picture? • **Pink** mouse says, "That person's face looks like a puzzle." • **Orange** mouse says, "I see a pretty lady dancing with a fan.

Pictures of people are called portraits. Artists try to reveal what the person they are painting is really like. They try to show how they look, how they act, how they feel. Sometimes people have to pose for a long time while their picture is being painted. At other tImes, artists paint from photographs or from memory.

Dancing makes me feel happy, too." • Beige mouse says, "The old woman in a chair looks really strict to me. I bet she doesn't even know how to laugh." • **Purple** mouse says, "That lady is dressed very elegantly, as if she is going to a fancy party." • The cat says, "If I could meet one person from these paintings, this is who it would be." Try to guess who it is.

Landscapes are pictures of all sorts of different outdoor places. Some of these paintings also include people in the scene. Many artists like to sketch and paint while they are outside. They look carefully and notice how the world is constantly changing with the weather, the season, and the time of day.

LANDSCAPES

Look at each picture and try to imagine being part of it, as if you are surrounded by nature. Can you describe where you are? Is it sunny or dark, wet or dry, windy or calm? Do you hear sounds, or is it completely quiet? How do you feel being in this place? • **Green** mouse says, "I'm imagining that I am in a peaceful place just like those two people." • **Orange** mouse

says, "I'd like to be in the cool, shaded woods, having a picnic." • **Brown** mouse says, "I want to be in the park by the river. I wish I could walk the monkey, too." • **Blue** mouse says, "I think it would be scary to be out in that storm." • The cat says, "I feel as if I'm a bird flying high in the sky over fields and ocean." Which painting makes her feel this way?

STILL LIFES

These paintings are filled with all kinds of different objects. Do you see fruit, flowers, vases, books? What else? Are some things easier to recognize than others? • Light Blue mouse says, "That fruit looks yummy. I love all kinds of fruit." • Red mouse says, "I hope no one sits down on that chair!" • Pink mouse says, "I think that is a jug and some fruit on a

table, but the artist has painted them so they are almost hidden in a design." • Yellow mouse says, "I like the vase of sunflowers. They look fresh, as if they've just been picked from a garden on a hot day." • The cat says, "Just looking at this painting makes me hungry." Which painting is that?

ABSTRACT ART

What are your favorite colors in these paintings? What shapes can you find—circles, triangles, squares? Any others? What kind of lines do you see—straight, curved, thick, or thin? As you look closely at the designs in the paintings, do they remind you of things you know? • Orange mouse says, "The shapes hanging from the ceiling look like fish, or maybe a giant

These paintings look more like designs of colors, shapes, and lines than pictures of real things. Some artists believe colors are like emotions, and that colors can be happy, angry, or sad. The artists try to show their feelings and experiences in new ways in their paintings. They may change what they see so much that it is hard to recognize in them anything from the real world.

spider." • **Purple** mouse says, "This painting makes me think of the night except the colors are mixed up." • **Red** mouse says, "The painting with the crisscrossing lines and bright colors reminds me of busy city streets." • The cat says, "These beautiful colors and fun, curvy shapes make me feel happy." Which painting makes her feel like this?

Many artists paint pictures that illustrate scenes from ancient stories, legends, and myths. Sometimes artists show characters they have read about in books. Sometimes they show creatures they have made up in their own imaginations. As if by magic, artists can bring these mermaids, unicorns, dragons, and fantastic creatures to life.

FANTASTIC CREATURES

What different creatures and characters do you see in these paintings? What are they like? Do they seem scary, brave, magical, mysterious? What do you think is happening? Do any of these pictures illustrate stories you know? Would you want to meet any of these creatures yourself? • Green mouse says, "That's a scary dragon. Why is that lady just

standing there?" • **Blue** mouse says, "That girl looks like the Little Mermaid from the fairy tale. I think she found some gold at the bottom of the ocean." • **Yellow** mouse says, "Maybe the unicorn is looking in the mirror because he thinks he is handsome." • The cat says, "It would be fun to meet creatures like this in real life." Guess which ones she is talking about.

In some of these pictures, artists show people sleeping. In others, artists have tried to show what dreams can be like. Have you ever tried to describe one of your dreams? Do you ever wonder what other people dream about? What is happening in these pictures? How do these pictures make you feel? • **Red** mouse says, "That man is growing an apple on his

When people fall asleep, they slip into the world of their dreams. Dreams can be strange, beautiful, or spooky. They can be filled with hidden and secret thoughts. They don't always make sense. Many artists have tried to capture the weird atmosphere of dreams, nightmares, and fantasies in their paintings.

face. He is funny-looking." • **Brown** mouse says, "I think the picture with the squishy, oozy clocks is kind of creepy." • **Orange** mouse says, "I like the gentle lion under the light of the moon. I wouldn't be scared if he was whispering to me." • The cat says, "My picture looks like a dream!" Do you see someone sleeping in her picture now?

Conclusion

The cat and the ten mice leave the museum together. Their visit is over, and it's time to go home. • **Red** mouse says, "I had so much fun." • Yellow mouse says, "I loved the painting with the three musicians." • Green mouse says, "We could form a band and make music together, too." • Pink mouse says, "I want to paint my own pictures." • **Brown** mouse says, "I'm just full of ideas." • Beige mouse says, "And things I

want to do." • Light Blue mouse says, "I feel great—as if everything is possible." • Purple mouse says, "Me, too." • Orange mouse says, "I want to be in the circus like the lady in my favorite painting. How about you?" • Blue mouse says, "I can't wait to visit again." • The cat says, "The museum is my favorite place to go. My dream was always to be an artist. Follow your own dreams, everyone."

LISTED BELOW are the works of art that inspired the pictures in the museum in this book. They are listed by gallery; the number next to each entry corresponds to the number in the sketch for each gallery. Each artwork is listed by name of artist / date of birth and death / title and date of painting (all are paintings unless otherwise noted) / location of the work of art.

ARTISTS

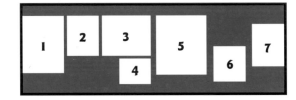

1 Diego Velázquez / 1599–1660 / *The Maids of Honor (Las meninas)*, 1656 / Prado, Madrid • **2** Marie-Denise Villers / 1774–1821 / *Young Woman Drawing*, ca. 1800 / Metropolitan Museum of Art, New York • **3** Henri Matisse / 1869–1954 / *The Red Studio*, 1911 / Museum of Modern Art, New York • **4** Vincent van Gogh / 1853–1890 / *Bedroom at Arles*, 1889 / Versions at Art Institute of Chicago and Musée d'Orsay, Paris • **5** Jan Vermeer / 1632–1675 / *The Art of Painting*, ca. 1666–67 / Kunsthistorisches Museum, Vienna • **6** Henri Matisse / 1869–1954 / *The Painter in His Studio*, 1916 / Musée National d'Art Moderne, Paris • **7** Vincent van Gogh / 1853–1890 / *Self-Portrait Before Easel*, 1888 / Van Gogh Museum, Amsterdam

MUSIC AND DANCE

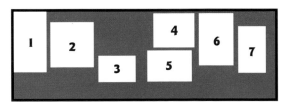

1 Édouard Manet / 1832–1883 / *The Fifer*, 1866 / Musée d'Orsay, Paris • **2** Henri Matisse / 1869–1954 / *Music*, 1939 / Albright-Knox Art Gallery, Buffalo, New York • **3** Pierre-Auguste Renoir / 1841–1919 / *The Daughters of Catulle Mendès*, 1888 / private collection • **4** Pablo Picasso / 1881–1973 / *Three Musicians*, 1921 / Museum of Modern Art, New York • **5** Henri Matisse / 1869–1954 / *Dance I*, 1909 / Museum of Modern Art, New York • **6** Georges Seurat / 1859–1891 / *The Circus*, 1891 / Musée d'Orsay, Paris • **7** Edgar Degas / 1834–1917 / *The Little Fourteen-Year-Old Dancer* (sculpture), 1880–81 / Copies at Metropolitan Museum of Art, New York; Tate Gallery, London; Musée d'Orsay, Paris; and elsewhere

CHILDREN PLAYING

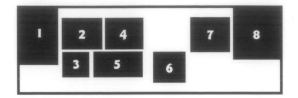

1 Giorgio de Chirico / 1888–1978 / *Mystery and Melancholy of a Street*, 1914 / private collection ○ **2** Balthus / 1908– / *The Game of Cards*, 1948–50 / Thyssen Collection ○ **3** Jean-Honoré Fragonard / 1732–1806 / *The Swing*, 1767 / Wallace Collection, London ○ **4** Paul Cézanne / 1839–1906 / *The Card Players*, 1893–96 / Versions at Courtauld Institute Galleries, London, and Musée d'Orsay, Paris ○ **5** Winslow Homer / 1836–1910 / *Snap the Whip*, 1872 / Versions at Metropolitan Museum of Art, New York, and Butler Institute of American Art, Youngstown, Ohio ○ **6** Pablo Picasso / 1881–1973 / *Bather with Beach Ball*, 1932 / Museum of Modern Art, New York ○ **7** Henri Matisse / 1869–1954 / *The Painter's Family*, 1911 / Hermitage Museum, St. Petersburg, Russia ○ **8** Pieter Bruegel the Elder / ca. 1525–1569 / *The Children's Games*, 1560 / Kunsthistorisches Museum, Vienna

CHILDREN AND PETS

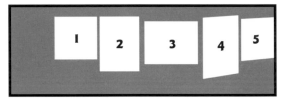

1 Ammi Phillips / 1788–1865 / *Girl in Red Dress with Cat and Dog*, ca. 1830–35 / Museum of American Folk Art, New York • **2** Francisco Goya / 1746–1828 / *Don Manuel Osorio Manrique de Zuñiga*, ca. 1788–92 / Metropolitan Museum of Art, New York • **3** William Hogarth / 1697–1764 / *The Graham Children*, 1742 / National Gallery, London • **4** Francisco Goya / 1746–1828 / *The Duchess of Alba*, 1797 / private collection • **5** Pablo Picasso / 1881–1973 / *Child Holding a Dove*, 1901 / National Gallery, London

PORTRAITS

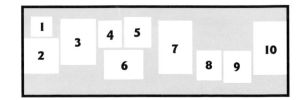

1 Paul Klee / 1879–1940 / *Senecio*, 1922 / Kunstmuseum, Basel, Switzerland • **2** Édouard Manet / 1832–1883 / *A Bar at the Folies-Bergère*, 1881–82 / Courtauld Institute Galleries, London • **3** Jan van Eyck / ca. 1390–1441 / *Giovanni Arnolfini and His Wife*, 1434 / National Gallery, London • **4** Edvard Munch / 1863–1944 / *The Scream*, 1893 / Nasjonalgalleriet, Oslo • **5** Pablo Picasso / 1881–1973 / *Woman at a Window*, 1936 / private collection • **6** James

Abbott McNeill Whistler / 1834–1903 / *Portrait of the Artist's Mother*, 1871 / Musée d'Orsay, Paris • **7** Claude Monet / 1840–1926 / *La Japonaise (Madame Monet in Japanese Costume)*, 1876 / Museum of Fine Arts, Boston • **8** Jan Vermeer / 1632–1675 / *Girl with a Pearl Earring*, 1665–66 / Mauritshuis, The Hague • **9** Leonardo da Vinci / 1452–1519 / *Mona Lisa*, 1503–6 / Louvre, Paris • **10** John Singer Sargent / 1856–1925 / *Portrait of Madame X (Madame Gautreau)*, 1884 / Metropolitan Museum of Art, New York

ABSTRACT ART

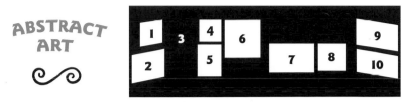

1 Piet Mondrian / 1872–1944 / *Composition with Red, Yellow, and Blue*, 1920 / Stedelijk Museum, Amsterdam • **2** Piet Mondrian /1872–1944 / *Broadway Boogie Woogie*, 1942–43 / Museum of Modern Art, New York • **3** Alexander Calder / 1898–1976 / *Hanging Spider* (sculpture), ca. 1940 / private collection • **4** Henri Matisse / 1869–1954 / *The Snail*, 1952–53 / Tate Gallery, London • **5** Paul Klee / 1879–1940 / *Park near Lucerne*, 1938 / Kunstmuseum, Bern, Switzerland • **6** Sonia Delaunay / 1885–1979 / *Electric Prisms*, 1914 / Musée National d'Art Moderne, Paris • **7** Joan Miró / 1893–1983 / *The Nightingale's Song at Midnight and Morning Rain*, 1940 / private collection • **8** Henri Matisse / 1869–1954 / *The Beasts of the Sea*, 1950 / National Gallery of Art, Washington, D.C. • **9** Wassily Kandinsky / 1866–1944 / *Cossacks*, 1910–11 / Tate Gallery, London • **10** Wassily Kandinsky / 1866–1944 / *Succession*, 1935 / Phillips Collection, Washington, D.C.

LANDSCAPES

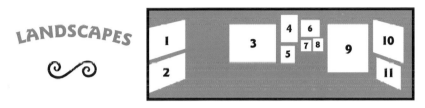

1 Victor Pasmore / 1908–1998 / *Spiral Motif in Green, Violet, Blue, and Gold: The Coast of the Inland Sea*, 1950 / Tate Gallery, London • **2** Thomas Gainsborough / 1727–1788 / *Mr. and Mrs. Andrews*, 1748–49 / National Gallery, London • **3** Édouard Manet / 1832–1883 / *Luncheon on the Grass*, 1862– 63 / Versions at Musée d'Orsay, Paris, and Courtauld Institute Galleries, London • **4** Claude Monet / 1840–1926 / *Water Lilies*, 1907 / Museum of Fine Arts, Boston • **5** Claude Monet / 1840–1926 / *Haystacks. Late Summer. Giverny*, 1891 / Musée d'Orsay, Paris • **6** Milton Avery / 1893–1965 / *Dunes and Sea II*, 1960 / Whitney Museum of American Art, New York • **7** Milton Avery / 1893–1965 / *Tangerine Moon and Wine Dark Sea*, 1959 / private collection • **8** Milton Avery / 1893–1965 / *Sea Grasses and Blue Sea*, 1958 / Museum of Modern Art, New York • **9** Georges Seurat / 1859–1891 / *A Sunday Afternoon on the Island of La Grande Jatte*, 1884–86 / Art Institute of Chicago • **10** Vincent van Gogh / 1853–1890 / *The Starry Night*, 1889 / Museum of Modern Art, New York • **11** Katsushika Hokusai / 1760–1849 / *The Great Wave at Kanagawa*, 1823–29 / Metropolitan Museum of Art, New York

FANTASTIC CREATURES

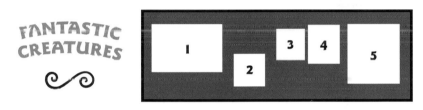

1 Paolo Uccello / 1397–1475 / *St. George and the Dragon*, ca. 1460 / National Gallery, London • **2** Edvard Eriksen / 1876–1959 / *The Little Mermaid* (sculpture), 1913 / Copenhagen Harbor • **3** Joan Miró / 1893–1983 / *Snob Party at the Princess's*, 1944 / private collection • **4** *Sphinx* (sculpture, Greek), ca. 530 B.C. / Metropolitan Museum of Art, New York • **5** *Sight*, detail from *The Lady with the Unicorn* (tapestry, southern Netherlands), 1480–90 / Musée de Cluny, Paris

STILL LIFES

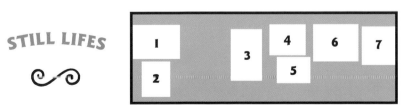

1 Paul Cézanne / 1839–1906 / *Apples and Oranges*, ca. 1895–1900 / Musée d'Orsay, Paris • **2** Vincent van Gogh / 1853–1890 / *Vincent's Chair*, 1888–89 / National Gallery, London • **3** Pablo Picasso / 1881–1973 / *Large Still Life on a Pedestal Table*, 1931 / Musée Picasso, Paris • **4** Giorgio Morandi / 1890–1964 / *Still Life*, 1946 / Tate Gallery, London • **5** Georges Braque / 1882–1963 / *The Black Fish*, 1942 / Musée National d'Art Moderne, Paris • **6** Henri Matisse / 1869–1954 / *Interior with a Dog / The Magnolia Branch*, 1934 / Baltimore Museum of Art, Baltimore • **7** Vincent van Gogh / 1853–1890 / *Sunflowers*, 1888 / Tate Gallery, London

SLEEPING AND DREAMING

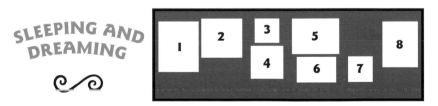

1 Pablo Picasso / 1881–1973 / *The Dream*, 1932 / private collection • **2** Salvador Dali / 1904–1989 / *The Persistence of Memory*, 1931 / Museum of Modern Art, New York • **3** René Magritte / 1898–1967 / *The Son of Man*, 1964 / private collection • **4** Henri Matisse / 1869–1954 / *The Dream*, 1939–40 / private collection • **5** Henri Rousseau / 1844–1910 / *The Sleeping Gypsy*, 1897 / Museum of Modern Art, New York • **6** Vincent van Gogh / 1853–1890 / *The Noonday Nap*, 1889–90 / Musée d'Orsay, Paris • **7** Marc Chagall / 1887–1985 / *Time Is a River Without Banks*, 1930–39 / Museum of Modern Art, New York • **8** René Magritte / 1898–1967 / *The Reckless Sleeper*, 1927 / Tate Gallery, London

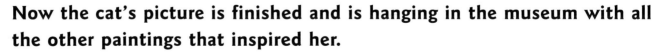

DREAMING OF ART
BY CAT

Now the cat's picture is finished and is hanging in the museum with all the other paintings that inspired her.

ARTISTS gallery: *Bedroom at Arles* by Vincent van Gogh • **MUSIC AND DANCE** gallery: *Music* by Henri Matisse • **CHILDREN PLAYING** gallery: *The Painter's Family* by Henri Matisse • **CHILDREN AND PETS** gallery: *Girl in Red Dress with Cat and Dog* by Ammi Phillips • **PORTRAITS** gallery: *Girl with a Pearl Earring* by Jan Vermeer • **LANDSCAPES** gallery: *Spiral Motif in Green, Violet, Blue, and Gold: The Coast of the Inland Sea* by Victor Pasmore • **STILL LIFES** gallery: *The Black Fish* by Georges Braque • **ABSTRACT ART** gallery: *The Beasts of the Sea* by Henri Matisse • **FANTASTIC CREATURES** gallery: *Snob Party at the Princess's* by Joan Miró • **SLEEPING AND DREAMING** gallery: *The Dream* by Henri Matisse